The Best of Closet Cooking 2017

By: Kevin Lynch

ClosetCooking.com

Table of Contents

Introduction

Hi! I am Kevin Lynch and I am the author of ClosetCooking.com, a food and recipe website, where I share my favourite recipes that I cook in my closet sized kitchen. For most of my life I did not really cook much of anything but all that changed a few years ago when I found my love of cooking and things kind of snow balled from there! These days cooking is my passion and I spend most of my free time in the kitchen whipping up tasty dishes that I photograph and share on ClosetCooking.com.

It has become a tradition for me to assemble the most popular recipes on ClosetCooking.com every year and place them in a cookbook. This is the 2018 edition of The Best of Closet Cooking series with all of the tastiest recipes published on ClosetCooking.com in 2017. The year 2017 was filled with plenty of tasty recipes and this collection of them is an amazing one filled with a lot of quick and easy meals, sides, soups and appetizers that that are on the healthier side along with some decadent recipes for tailgating or special occasions! For your gastronomic pleasure I give you the 25 tastiest and most popular recipes from ClosetCooking.com in 2017 in order of popularity!

Enjoy!

Kevin Lynch

Roasted Mushrooms in a Browned Butter, Garlic and Thyme Sauce

Prep Time: 5 minutes **Cook Time**: 25 minutes
Total Time: 30 minutes **Servings**: 4

Roasted mushrooms tossed in a tasty browned butter, garlic and thyme sauce!

ingredients
1 pound mushrooms, cleaned
1 tablespoon oil
salt and pepper to taste
1/4 cup butter
2 cloves garlic, chopped
1 teaspoon thyme, chopped
1 tablespoon lemon juice
salt and pepper to taste

directions
1. Toss the mushrooms in the oil, salt and pepper, place on a baking sheet in a single layer and roast in a preheated 400F/200C oven until they start to caramelize, about 20 minutes, mixing half way through.
2. Cook the butter over medium heat in a sauce pan until it starts to turn a nice hazelnut brown, remove from heat and mix in the garlic, thyme and lemon juice.
3. Toss the roasted mushrooms in the browned butter and season with salt and pepper to taste!

Nutrition Facts: Calories 109 , Fat 9.5g (Saturated 4.1g, Trans 0g), Cholesterol 15mg, Sodium 49mg, Carbs 4g (Fiber 1g, Sugars 2g), Protein 3.8g

Balsamic Garlic Grilled Mushroom Skewers

Prep Time: 10 minutes **Marinate Time**: 30 minutes
Cook Time: 10 minutes **Total Time**: 20 minutes
Servings: 4

Smoky grilled balsamic and garlic marinated mushroom skewers!

ingredients
2 pounds mushrooms, sliced 1/4 inch thick
2 tablespoons balsamic vinegar
1 tablespoon soy sauce (or tamari)
3 cloves garlic, chopped
1/2 teaspoon thyme, chopped
salt and pepper to taste

directions
1. Marinate the mushrooms in the mixture of the remaining ingredients for 30 minutes or longer.
2. Skewer the mushrooms and grill over medium-high heat until just tender and slightly charred, about 2-3 minutes per side.

Nutrition Facts: Calories 62, Fat 0.8g (Saturated 0, Trans 0), Cholesterol 0, Sodium 233mg, Carbs 9g (Fiber 2g, Sugars 5g), Protein 7g

Slow Cooker Balsamic Glazed Roast Beef

Prep Time: 10 minutes **Cook Time**: 8 hours 30 minutes
Total Time: 8 hours 40 minutes **Servings**: 8

Moist and fall apart tender roast beef in a tasty balsamic glaze that is so easy to make in the slow cooker!

ingredients
1 tablespoon oil
3 pounds roasting beef such as chuck, round, brisket
1 large onion, sliced
4 cloves garlic, chopped
1/2 teaspoon red pepper flakes
1 cup beef broth
1/2 cup balsamic vinegar
2 tablespoons soy sauce (or tamari)
2 tablespoons brown sugar
1 tablespoon Worcestershire sauce
1 pound baby carrots (optional)
1 pound mini potatoes or diced potatoes (optional)
2 tablespoons cornstarch mixed into 2 tablespoons
   cool water

directions
1. Heat the oil in a large pan over medium-high heat, add the beef and brown on all sides, about 20 minutes and set aside.
2. Add the onions and cook until tender, about 2-3 minutes, before adding the garlic and red pepper flakes and cooking until fragrant, about a minute.
3. Place the beef, onions, broth, balsamic vinegar, soy sauce, brown sugar, Worcestershire sauce, carrots and potatoes in a slow cooker, cover and cook on low for 8-10 hours or on high for 3-5 hours. (The beef will be falling apart tender when done!)
4. Remove the carrots, potatoes and beef and slice or shred the beef.
5. Skim any fat from the cooking juices, place it in a sauce pan, bring to a simmer, add the mixture of the cornstarch and water and cook until the glaze has thickened a bit.

Option: Skip steps 1 and 2 and just place everything into the slow cooker!
Option: Instead of transferring to a slow cooker in step 3, place everything in the pot that you cooked the beef in, bring to a boil, reduce the heat and simmer, covered, until the meat is pull apart tender, about 3-4 hours. OR Transfer the pot to a preheated 275F and braise until the meat is pull apart tender, about 3-4 hours.

Nutrition Facts: Calories 524, Fat 33.6g (Saturated 12.3g, Trans 0), Cholesterol 116mg, Sodium 464mg, Carbs 20.9g (Fiber 3.5g, Sugars 6.9g), Protein 32.2g

Slow Cooker Balsamic Roast Beef French Dip Sandwich

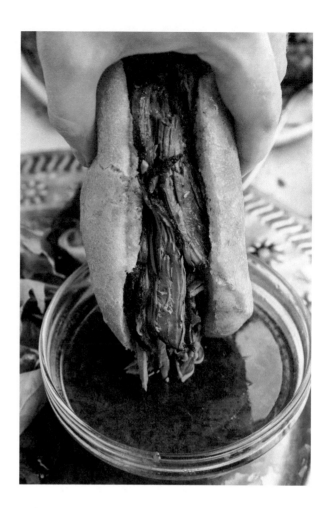

Prep Time: 5 minutes **Cook Time**: 5 minutes
Total Time: 10 minutes **Servings**: 4

Easy slow cooker balsamic roast beef french dip sandwiches where the roast beef is served in a bun along with the juices from the roast for dipping the sandwich into!

ingredients
4 buns (gluten-free for gluten-free)
2 cups slow cooker balsamic glazed roast beef (warm)
1/2 cup onions from slow cooker balsamic glazed roast beef (warm)
4 slices swiss cheese (optional)
1 cup juices from slow cooker balsamic glazed roast beef (warm)

directions
1. Assemble the sandwiches with the roast beef, onions and cheese, optionally baking to melt the cheese, and serve with juices for dipping!

Option: Add 1 tablespoon red miso paste to the dipping sauce!

Nutrition Facts: Calories 370, Fat 12.2g (Saturated 5.4g, Trans 0), Cholesterol 102mg, Sodium 302mg, Carbs 23.1g (Fiber 1.4g, Sugars 3.9g), Protein 38g

Balsamic Honey and Mustard Pork Chops

Prep Time: 5 minutes **Marinate Time**: 30 minutes
Cook Time: 10 minutes **Total Time**: 45 minutes
Servings: 4

Juicy pork chops in a tasty balsamic, honey and mustard sauce with a hint of blackberries that are so quick and easy to make and so tasty that you'll be making them all the time!

ingredients
1 pound pork chops
1/4 cup balsamic vinegar
1/4 cup honey
1/4 cup blackberry jam
2 tablespoons dijon mustard
1 tablespoon sriracha (or to taste)
1 tablespoon soy sauce (or tamari or omit for gluten-free)
2 cloves garlic, chopped
1 tablespoon oil

directions
1. Marinate the pork chops in the mixture of the balsamic vinegar, honey, blackberry jam, mustard, sriracha, soy sauce and garlic for 30 minutes to overnight.
2. Heat the oil in a large pan over medium-high heat, add the pork chops and cook until lightly golden brown on one side, about 3-5 minutes, flip them, add the marinade and cook until sauce has thickened and the pork chops are done, about 3-5 minutes.

Option: Replace the blackberry jam with another jam like strawberry or apricot or omit it entirely.

Nutrition Facts: Calories 366, Fat 14g (Saturated 3g, Trans 0), Cholesterol 78mg, Sodium 471mg, Carbs 34g (Fiber 0.5g, Sugars 29g), Protein 24g

Blackberry Balsamic Grilled Chicken Salad with Crispy Fried Goat Cheese

Prep Time: 10 minutes **Marinate Time**: 30 minutes
Cook Time: 10 minutes **Total Time**: 20 minutes
Servings: 4

Blackberry and balsamic marinated grilled chicken and black berry salad with crispy fried goat cheese and avocado!

ingredients

FOR THE BLACKBERRY BALSAMIC VINAIGRETTE DRESSING:

1/2 cup blackberries
2 tablespoons white balsamic vinegar
2 tablespoons extra virgin olive oil
2 tablespoons honey
2 teaspoons Dijon mustard
1 teaspoon tamari or soy sauce
1 large clove garlic, minced
salt and pepper to taste

FOR THE FRIED GOAT CHEESE:

8 ounces goat cheese, either sliced into 1/4 inch
    thick discs or formed into small balls
1/4 cup all-purpose flour (or rice flour for gluten free)
1 large egg, lightly beaten
1 cup panko breadcrumbs (or breadcrumbs; gluten-free for gluten-free)

FOR THE SALAD:

1/2 pound chicken breasts
6 cups salad greens, optionally sliced or torn
1 cup blackberries
1 avocado, sliced
1/4 cup red onion, sliced
1/4 cup walnuts (or pistachios or almonds)

directions

FOR THE BLACKBERRY BALSAMIC VINAIGRETTE DRESSING:

1. Mix everything well.

FOR THE FRIED GOAT CHEESE:

2. Dredge the goat cheese slices/balls in the flour and coat in egg followed by breadcrumbs and fry in oil over medium heat until lightly golden brown before setting aside on paper towels to drain.

FOR THE SALAD:

3. Marinate the chicken in half of the vinaigrette for 30 minutes to over night before grilling over medium-high heat until cooked and slightly charred, about 2-5 minutes per side, and setting aside to cool and slice.

4. Assemble the salad and enjoy!

Option: Add sriracha to taste to the dressing.
Option: Add prosciutto or crispy bacon!
Note: Best enjoyed while the fried goat cheese is still warm from frying!

Nutrition Facts: Calories 631, Fat 35g (Saturated 12g, Trans 0), Cholesterol 108mg, Sodium 633mg, Carbs 48g (Fiber 8g, Sugars 15g), Protein 31g

Melting Potatoes

Prep Time: 10 minutes **Cook Time**: 35 minutes
Total Time: 45 minutes **Servings**: 4

Magical roasted potatoes that are crispy on the outside and melt in your mouth on the inside served in a tasty lemon and garlic sauce!

ingredients

1 1/2 pounds yellow fleshed potatoes (such as Yukon gold), peeled and sliced 1 inch thick
4 tablespoons butter, melted
1 teaspoon thyme, chopped
salt and pepper to taste
1 cup chicken broth or vegetable broth
1 tablespoon lemon juice (optional)
2 garlic cloves, lightly crushed and peeled

directions

1. Toss the potatoes in the mixture of the butter, thyme, salt and pepper, arrange in a single layer in a baking pan and bake in a preheated 500F/260C oven on the top-middle rack until golden brown, about 10-15 minutes, per side.
2. Flip the potatoes again, add the broth, lemon juice and garlic and roast for another 10 minutes

Option: Sprinkle on some crumbled feta while they are still hot from the oven!

Nutrition Facts: Calories 176, Fat 6g (Saturated 3.7, Trans 0), Cholesterol 15mg, Sodium 69mg, Carbs 27.3g (Fiber 4.3g, Sugars 2.1g), Protein 3.7g

Apricot Glazed Bacon Wrapped Cajun Pork Tenderloin

Prep Time: 5 minutes **Cook Time**: 25 minutes
Total Time: 30 minutes **Servings**: 4

A moist and juicy cajun seasoned pork tenderloin wrapped in crispy bacon and glazed in an apricot dijon sauce! Sweet and salty pork perfection!

ingredients
1 1/2 pound pork tenderloin
1 tablespoon cajun seasoning
1/4 cup brown sugar
6 strips bacon
3 tablespoons apricot preserves
1 tablespoon grainy dijon mustard

directions
1. Rub the pork tenderloin with the mixture of the cajun seasoning and brown sugar and wrap it up in the bacon (optionally pinning with toothpicks).
2. Heat an oven safe skillet over medium heat, add the bacon wrapped pork tenderloin and cook until it is browned on all sides, about 10-15 minutes.
3. Transfer the pan to a preheated 400F/200C oven, roast until the pork reaches 140F, about 10-15 minutes, brushing on the mixture of the apricot preserves and mustard near the end before setting aside it to rest, covered, for 5 minutes, and slicing.

Nutrition Facts: Calories 361, Fat 10.2g (Saturated 3.4g, Trans 0), Cholesterol 135mg, Sodium 619mg, Carbs 15.2g (Fiber 0, Sugars 11.3g), Protein 48.8g

Honey Sriracha Roasted Carrots

Prep Time: 5 minutes **Cook Time**: 15 minutes
Total Time: 20 minutes **Servings**: 4

These honey sriracha roasted carrots are a tasty, quick and easy side dish for any meal!

ingredients

2 pounds carrots, cleaned and sliced 1/4+ inch thick
1 tablespoon honey
1 tablespoon sriracha (or other chili sauce)
1 tablespoon oil
salt and pepper to taste

directions

1. Toss the carrots in the mixture of the honey, sriracha, oil, salt and pepper, arrange in a single layer on a baking sheet and bake in a preheated 400F/200C oven until tender, about 15-20 minutes, turning once in the middle. (Tip: Don't pour any excess honey and sriracha onto the baking sheet as it will just burn; save it and toss the roasted carrots in it before serving.)

Nutrition Facts: Calories 118, Fat 1.7g (Saturated 0, Trans 0), Cholesterol 0, Sodium 169mg, Carbs 26g (Fiber 6g, Sugars 13.3g), Protein 2g

Grilled Chicken and Asparagus Caprese Spinach Salad with Bacon and Avocado

Prep Time: 10 minutes **Cook Time**: 20 minutes
Total Time: 30 minutes **Servings**: 4

A hearty grilled chicken and asparagus spinach 'caprese' salad with tomatoes, mozzarella, basil and a balsamic vinaigrette along with bacon and avocado!

ingredients

1/2 pound boneless and skinless chicken breast
salt and pepper to taste
1 pound asparagus, washed and trimmed
salt and pepper to taste
1 tablespoon oil
4 strips bacon, cut into 1/2 inch pieces
6 cups baby spinach, washed
8 ounces tomatoes, diced
8 ounces mini bocconcini or mozzarella balls
1 large avocado, diced
1/4 balsamic vinaigrette
1/4 cup basil, sliced

directions

1. Season the chicken with salt and pepper and grill or pan fry over medium-high heat until cooked, about 3-5 minutes per side before setting aside.
2. Toss the asparagus spears in the oil, salt and pepper and grill or pan fry over medium-high heat until crisp-tender and slightly charred before setting aside to cool and slicing into bite sized pieces.
3. Meanwhile, cook the bacon until crispy and set aside on paper to towels to drain.
4. Assemble the salad, toss and enjoy!

Option: Make this a one-pan meal by cooking the bacon in a pan, followed by the chicken (instead of on the grill), followed by the asparagus.
Option: Cook the bacon before hand to speed things up and to allow you to do all of the cooking at the grill.

Nutrition Facts: Calories 380, Fat 23g (Saturated 8g, Trans 0), Cholesterol 62mg, Sodium 501mg, Carbs 14.3g (Fiber 7.4g, Sugars 4.2g), Protein 32.8g

Rustic Roasted Garlic Chicken with Asiago Gravy

Prep Time: 5 minutes **Cook Time**: 25 minutes
Total Time: 30 minutes **Servings**: 4

A rustic one-pan roast chicken with whole cloves of garlic in a super tasty asiago gravy!

ingredients

1 tablespoon oil
4 (6 ounce) bone-in, skin on chicken thighs
salt and pepper to taste
1 onion, diced
20 cloves garlic, peeled
2 teaspoons fresh thyme, chopped (or 1 teaspoon dry thyme)
2 tablespoons flour (rice flour for gluten-free)
1 cups chicken broth
1/2 cup asiago cheese (or parmesan), grated
salt and pepper to taste

directions

1. Heat the oil in a large pan over medium-high heat, add the chicken (seasoned with salt and pepper) and brown, abut 3-5 minutes per side, before setting aside.
2. Add the onion and garlic and saute until the onions are tender and the everything is lightly browned, about 3-5 minutes.
3. Sprinkle in the thyme and flour and cook for a minute.
4. Add the broth and deglaze the pan by scraping the brown bits off of the bottom of the pan with a spoon while the broth is sizzling when added.
5. Mix the asiago into the sauce and season with salt and pepper to taste.
6. Add the chicken, cover (with a lid or foil) and roast in a preheated 400F/200C oven for 15 minutes OR turn the heat down to medium-low and simmer, covered, on the stove top for 15 minutes.

Slow Cooker: Optionally (and highly recommended) implement steps 1-5, place everything in the slow cooker and cook on low for 4-10 hours or high for 2-4 hours. If you skip the earlier steps, whisk the flour into the broth before mixing in the slow cooker.
Option: Make this a one-pan meal by adding 8 ounces of pasta and 2 1/4 cups broth or water (or 1 cup of rice and 2 cups broth or water) to the sauce in step 8 and simmer, covered, until cooked, about 12 minutes (or 20 minutes for rice).
Option: Add 1 tablespoons white miso paste to the sauce! (Do it if you have it!)
Option: Add a splash of lemon juice to the sauce!
Option: Add 1/2 cup heavy/whipping cream to the sauce!
Option: Add 1/2 pound sliced mushrooms along with the onions!
Option: Add diced potatoes and carrots to the pan before placing the chicken on top and roasting until the veggies are tender, about 20-30 minutes!

Nutrition Facts: Calories 524, Fat 33.6g (Saturated 12.3g, Trans 0), Cholesterol 116mg, Sodium 464mg, Carbs 20.9g (Fiber 3.5g, Sugars 6.9g), Protein 32.2g

Creamy Lemon Grilled Chicken, Asparagus and Artichoke Pasta

Prep Time: 10 minutes **Cook Time**: 20 minutes
Total Time: 30 minutes **Servings**: 4

A bright and fresh grilled chicken and asparagus pasta in a creamy lemon and artichoke sauce!

ingredients

1/2 pound boneless and skinless chicken breast
salt and pepper to taste
1 pound asparagus, washed and trimmed
salt and pepper to taste
1 tablespoon oil
8 ounce fettuccine (gluten-free for gluten-free)
1 tablespoon butter
2 cloves garlic, chopped
4 ounces cream cheese (reduced fat is ok), room
    temperature, cubed
1/2 cup parmigiano reggiano (parmesan), grated
1 cup milk (or broth or pasta water)
1 (14 ounce) can artichoke hearts, coarsely chopped
1 lemon, juice and zest
2 tablespoons parsley, chopped
salt and pepper to taste

directions

1. Season the chicken with salt and pepper and grill or pan fry over medium-high heat until cooked, about 3-5 minutes per side before setting aside.
2. Toss the asparagus spears in the oil, salt and pepper and grill or pan fry over medium-high heat until crisp-tender and slightly charred before setting aside to cool and slicing into bite sized pieces.
3. Meanwhile, cook the pasta as directed on the package.
4. Meanwhile melt the butter in a pan over medium heat, add the garlic and cook until fragrant, about a minute.
5. Add the cream cheese and let it melt before mixing in the parmesan, milk and artichokes and cooking until all of the cheese has melted.
6. Mix in the lemon juice and zest, parsley, season with salt and pepper to taste and enjoy!

Option: : Make this a one-pan meal by pan searing the chicken and asparagus in the pan instead of grilling and adding 1 1/4 cups water or chicken broth or milk with 8 ounces of pasta or 1 cup rice along with the other ingredients in step 5, covering and simmering until the pasta or rice is cooked, about 12 minutes for pasta or 20 minutes for the rice.

Option: Add red pepper flakes to taste with the garlic for some heat!

Nutrition Facts: Calories 462, Fat 14.9g (Saturated 7.2g, Trans 0), Cholesterol 105mg, Sodium 373mg, Carbs 55.4g (Fiber 11.3g, Sugars 7.3g), Protein 33.2g

Maple Roasted Carrots in Tahini Sauce with Pomegranate and Pistachios

Prep Time: 10 minutes **Cook Time**: 20 minutes
Total Time: 30 minutes **Servings**: 4

Sweet maple roasted carrots served topped with a tasty tahini sauce, pomegranate and pistachios!

ingredients

2 pounds carrots, cleaned and trimmed
1 tablespoon oil
1 tablespoon maple syrup
2 tablespoons tahini
2 tablespoons lemon juice
1 teaspoon white miso paste (or soy sauce or tamari for gluten-free; or salt)
1 teaspoon maple syrup
1 small clove garlic, grated
2 tablespoons water*
2 tablespoons pomegranate
2 tablespoons pistachios, chopped
1 tablespoon parsley or cilantro, chopped

directions

1. Toss the carrots in the mixture of the oil and maple syrup, arrange in a single layer on a baking sheet and roast in a preheated 400F/200C oven until tender, about 20-30 minutes, turning once in the middle.
2. Mix the tahini, lemon juice, miso, maple syrup, garlic and enough water to get the sauce to the desired consistency.
3. Serve the carrots topped with the tahini sauce, pomegranate, pistachios and parsley and enjoy!

Option: Replace maple syrup with honey.

Nutrition Facts: Calories 188, Fat 6.8g (Saturated 1g, Trans 0), Cholesterol 0, Sodium 221mg, Carbs 30g (Fiber 6.6g, Sugars 16g), Protein 4g

Asparagus and Lemon and Basil Ricotta Stuffed Salmon Rolls with Lemon Sauce

Prep Time: 15 minutes **Cook Time**: 15 minutes
Total Time: 30 minutes **Servings**: 4

Salmon rolls stuffed with a light lemon and basil ricotta along with asparagus that is baked and served with a fresh and tasty lemon sauce!

ingredients
4 (5 ounce) salmon fillets, skins removed
salt and pepper to taste
1 (12 ounce) container ricotta
1/2 cup parmigiano reggiano (parmesan), grated
2 tablespoons basil, chopped
2 teaspoons lemon zest
salt and pepper to taste
1/2 pound asparagus, trimmed
1 tablespoon butter
1/2 cup chicken broth
2 tablespoons lemon juice
2 teaspoons cornstarch

directions
1. Season the salmon fillets with salt and pepper to taste, lay them down with the skin side up, top with the mixture of the ricotta, parmesan, basil, lemon zest, salt and pepper, several spears of asparagus and roll them up before placing them on a greased baking sheet with the seam side down.
2. Bake in a preheated 425F/220C oven until the salmon is just cooked, about 15-20 minutes.
3. Meanwhile, melt the butter in a small sauce pan over medium heat, add the mixture of the broth, lemon juice and corn starch and heat until it thickens, about 3-5 minutes.
4. Serve the salmon rolls topped with the lemon sauce and optionally garnish with more basil and lemon zest.

Option: Replace the salmon with trout.
Option: Serve topped with asparagus pesto (next)!
Option: Serve in basil marinara sauce instead of the lemon sauce!

Nutrition Facts: Calories 400, Fat 21.7g (Saturated 9.4g, Trans 0), Cholesterol 107mg, Sodium 419mg, Carbs 8.8g (Fiber 1.3g, Sugars 1.6g), Protein 43.8g

Asparagus Pesto

Prep Time: 5 minutes **Cook Time**: 5 minutes
Total Time: 5 minutes
Servings: 16 (~1 cup or 16 1 tablespoon servings)

A light, fresh and bright asparagus and basil pesto!

ingredients
1 cup asparagus, blanched
1/2 cup basil
1 clove garlic
2 tablespoons pine nuts, toasted
4 tablespoons parmigiano reggiano (parmesan),
    grated
3 tablespoons olive oil
1/2 lemon, zest and juice
salt and pepper to taste

directions
1. Puree everything in a food processor.

Nutrition Facts: Calories 38, Fat 4g (Saturated 0.9g,
    Trans 0), Cholesterol 2mg, Sodium 17mg,
    Carbs 0.7g (Fiber 0.3g, Sugars 0.2g), Protein 1g

Bacon and Cheese Corned Beef Burger with Guinness Caramelized Onions

Prep Time: 5 minutes **Cook Time**: 1 hour 10 minutes
Total Time: 1 hour 15 minutes **Servings**: 4

Tasty corned beef burgers topped with Guinness caramelized onions and melted cheese along with bacon and a fried egg!

ingredients
1 tablespoon oil
1 large onion, sliced
1 cup Guinness (or beef broth)
1 teaspoon Worcestershire sauce
2 teaspoons grainy mustard
8 strips bacon
1 1/2 pounds corned beef, ground in food processor
4 slices white cheddar (or swiss) cheese
4 eggs
4 buns

directions
1. Heat the oil in a pan over medium heat.
2. Add the onions and saute until tender, about 5-7 minutes.
3. Add 1/4 cup Guinness , cover and simmer until the liquid has mostly evaporated, about 15 minutes and repeat three more times.
4. Remove from heat and mix in the Worcestershire sauce and grainy mustard.
5. Meanwhile, cook the bacon in a pan and set it aside on paper towels to drain.
6. Form the ground corned beef into 4 patties and grill or pan fry over medium-high heat or broil until cooked, about 3-5 minutes per side, topping with the cheese.
7. Fry the eggs, assemble the burgers and enjoy!

Nutrition Facts: Calories 727, Fat 45.6g (Saturated 19g, Trans 0g), Cholesterol 313mg, Sodium 2264mg, Carbs 26g (Fiber 1g, Sugars 5g), Protein 44.5g

Spinach and Artichoke Skillet Chicken with Sundried Tomatoes

Prep Time: 10 minutes **Cook Time**: 20 minutes
Total Time: 30 minutes **Servings**: 4

A quick and easy, one-pan spinach and artichoke chicken with sundried tomatoes! All of the flavours of spinach and artichoke dip in a light and tasty chicken dinner!

ingredients

1 tablespoon oil*
4 (6 ounce) skinless and boneless chicken breasts, pounded thin
salt and pepper to taste
2 cloves garlic, chopped
1/4 teaspoon red pepper flakes (optional)
1 cup chicken broth or chicken stock
1 (8 ounce) package reduced fat cream cheese, room temperature and cut into cubes
4 cups baby spinach
1 (14 ounce) can artichoke hearts, quartered or coarsely chopped
1/4 cup parmigiano reggiano (parmesan) cheese, grated
1/4 cup sun dried tomatoes, sliced

directions

1. Heat the oil in a pan over medium-high heat, season the chicken with salt and pepper, add the chicken to the pan and cook until lightly golden brown on both sides and cooked through, about 3-5 minutes per side, before setting aside.
2. Add the garlic and red pepper flakes to the pan and saute until fragrant, about a minute.
3. Add the broth and deglaze the pan by scraping the brown bits off of the bottom of the pan with a spoon while the broth is sizzling when added.
4. Reduce the heat to medium, add the cream cheese and cook, stirring, until the cream cheese has melted, about 2-4 minutes.
5. Add the spinach, artichokes, parmesan, sundried tomatoes and chicken and cook unit the spinach has melted before enjoying!

Option: : Make this a one-pan meal by adding 8 ounces of pasta and 2 1/4 cups broth or water (or 1 cup of rice and 2 cups broth or water) to the sauce in step 4 and simmer, covered, until cooked, about 12 minutes (or 20 minutes for rice).
Note: When I am using oil packed sundried tomatoes like in this recipe I like to use the oil from the jar whenever possible to add even more flavour!
Option: Add shredded mozzarella for an even cheesier sauce!

Nutrition Facts: Calories 447, Fat 17.6g (Saturated 7.4g, Trans 0), Cholesterol 163mg, Sodium 826mg, Carbs 18g (Fiber 6g, Sugars 5g), Protein 64.6g

Creamy Garlic and Brie Mushrooms

Prep Time: 5 minutes **Cook Time**: 15 minutes
Total Time: 20 minutes **Servings**: 4

A decadently creamy garlic and brie mushroom dish that is so quick and easy to make!

ingredients
1 tablespoon butter (or oil)
1 pound mushrooms
2 cloves garlic, chopped
1/4 cup vegetable broth or chicken broth
4 ounces brie (casings optionally removed), diced
salt and pepper to taste

directions
1. Melt the butte in a pan over medium heat, add the mushrooms and cook until they are tender and release their liquids, about 10-15 minutes.
2. Add the garlic and cook until fragrant, about a minute.
3. Add the broth and brie and cook until the brie has melted before seasoning with salt and pepper to taste.

Option: Add 1 teaspoon chopped thyme along with the garlic.
Option: Add 1/4 cup cooked crumbled bacon!
Option: Top with 1/2 cup panko breadcrumbs mixed with 2 tablespoons of melted butter and 1/4 cup grated parmesan and broil until lightly golden brown and crispy!

Nutrition Facts: Calories 152, Fat 11g (Saturated 5g, Trans 0), Cholesterol 28mg, Sodium 186mg, Carbs 4g (Fiber 1g, Sugars 2g), Protein 9g

Maple Pecan Melting Sweet Potatoes

Prep Time: 5 minutes **Cook Time**: 35 minutes
Total Time: 40 minutes **Servings**: 6

Crispy on the outside, melt in your mouth on the inside sweet potatoes covered in a maple pecan sauce!

ingredients

1 1/2 pounds sweet potatoes, peeled and cut into 1 inch thick discs
4 tablespoons butter, melted
1/4 teaspoon salt
1/2 cup maple syrup
1/2 cup pecans, coarsely chopped

directions

1. Toss the sweet potatoes in the butter and salt, place in a single layer on a metal baking sheet, and bake in a preheated 425F/220C oven until golden brown and crispy on both sides, about 15-20 minutes per side.
2. Meanwhile, bring the maple syrup to a simmer in a small sauce pan over medium heat, add the pecans, bring back to a simmer and remove from heat.

Option: Add 1 teaspoon vanilla to the sauce.
Option: Add 1/2 teaspoon of coarse sea salt to the sauce!
Option: Add a pinch of cinnamon to the sauce!

Nutrition Facts: Calories 453, Fat 22g (Saturated 8.4, Trans 0), Cholesterol 31mg, Sodium 246mg, Carbs 62.7g (Fiber 8.5g, Sugars 13.1g), Protein 4.2g

Cilantro Lime Shrimp Scampi with Zucchini Noodles

Prep Time: 10 minutes **Cook Time**: 10 minutes
Total Time: 20 minutes **Servings**: 4

Shrimp in a tasty butter, garlic and lime sauce with plenty of fresh cilantro/coriander served on zucchini noodles!

ingredients
2 tablespoons butter
1 pound jumbo shrimp (16-24), shelled and deveined
4 cloves garlic, chopped
1 pinch red pepper flakes (optional)
1/4 cup white wine or chicken broth or shrimp broth or vegetable broth
2 tablespoons lime juice (~1 lime)
3 medium zucchini, cut into noodles
salt and pepper to taste
1 teaspoon lime zest (~1 lime)
2 tablespoons cilantro, chopped

directions
1. Melt the butter in a pan over medium-high heat until frothy, add the shrimp, cook for 2 minutes, flip, add the garlic and red pepper flakes and cook for 1 more minute before setting the shrimp aside.
2. Add the white wine and lime juice to the pan, deglaze it, simmer for 2 minutes, add the zucchini noodles and cook until just tender, about 2 minutes, before seasoning with salt and pepper, adding the shrimp, lime zest and cilantro, tossing everything and removing from the heat.

Note: Cut the zucchini into noodles with a mandoline or a spiralizer.

Nutrition Facts: Calories 170, Fat 7g (Saturated 4g, Trans 0.3g), Cholesterol 158mg, Sodium 656mg, Carbs 7g (Fiber 1g, Sugars 3g), Protein 17g

Hot Melted Caprese Dip

Prep Time: 5 minutes **Cook Time**: 15 minutes
Total Time: 20 minutes **Servings**: 4

A hot melted cheese dip with tomatoes and basil pesto!

ingredients
1 pint cherry tomatoes, halved
16 ounces fresh mozzarella, cut into cubes
1/2 cup basil pesto
salt and pepper to taste

directions
1. Mix everything, place in a baking dish and bake in a preheated 425F/220C oven until the cheese is melted, bubbling on the sides and lightly golden brown on top, about 15-20 minutes.

Nutrition Facts: Calories 475,
    Fat 33.4g (Saturated 14g, Trans 0), Cholesterol 68mg,
    Sodium 883mg, Carbs 9g (Fiber 2g, Sugars 3g),
    Protein 36.1g

Candied Jalapenos

Prep Time: 10 minutes **Cook Time**: 10 minutes
Total Time: 20 minutes
Servings: 64 (4 cups or 64 1 tablespoon servings)

Sweet, tangy and spicy candied jalapenos, aka cowboy candy.

ingredients
3 pounds jalapeno peppers, sliced into 1/8-1/4 inch slices
6 cloves garlic, thinly sliced
2 cups cider vinegar
3 cups granulated sugar
2 teaspoons coriander seeds
1 teaspoon celery seed

directions
1. Bring the everything to a boil, reduce the heat and simmer for 5 minutes.

Note: Store in a sealed container in the fridge for up to 3 months.
Option: Use proper canning procedures to store longer.

Nutrition Facts: Calories 12, Fat 0 (Saturated 0, Trans 0), Cholesterol 0, Sodium 1mg, Carbs 2.2g (Fiber 0.6g, Sugars 1.5g), Protein 0.2g

Chocolate Covered Strawberry Brownies

Prep Time: 10 minutes **Cook Time**: 20 minutes
Cool Time: 30 minutes **Total Time**: 1 hour **Servings**: 9

Chocolate covered strawberry topped fudge-y brownies!

ingredients

1/2 cup (1 stick) butter
8 ounces semi-sweet chocolate, coarsely chopped
3/4 cup granulated sugar
2 large eggs
1 teaspoon vanilla extract
1/2 cup all-purpose flour
1 tablespoon baking powder
1/4 teaspoon salt
1 pound strawberries, sliced
8 ounces semi-sweet chocolate, coarsely chopped

directions

1. Melt the chocolate into the butter in a sauce pan over medium heat and let cool.
2. Mix the sugar and the eggs and mix into the cooled chocolate.
3. Sift the flour, baking powder and salt and mix into the chocolate mixture.
4. Pour the batter into a greased (optionally foil lined) 8x8 inch baking pan and bake in a preheated 350F/180C oven until a toothpick pushed into the center comes out clean, about 20-25 minutes.
5. Sprinkle the strawberries on top of the brownies.
6. Melt the chocolate over medium-low heat on the stove (or in a microwave), pour it over the strawberries and let cool until the chocolate is set, about 30-60 minutes.

Option: Add 2 tablespoons cocoa powder to the flour mixture. (For an even deeper chocolate flavour!)
Option: Add 1 teaspoon finely ground coffee to the flour mixture. (The coffee brings out or enhances the chocolate flavour!)
Option: Replace the butter with coconut oil.
Option: Replace the flour with rice flour or a gluten-free flout mix for gluten-free.

Nutrition Facts: Calories 456, Fat 26g (Saturated 15g, Trans 0.3g), Cholesterol 68mg, Sodium 209mg, Carbs 58g (Fiber 4g, Sugars 46g), Protein 4g

Lemon Chicken Orzo Soup

Prep Time: 10 minutes **Cook Time**: 20 minutes
Total Time: 30 minutes **Servings**: 4

A quick and easy homemade chicken and orzo soup that is nice, light and satisfying and just packed with the brightness of summer with the fresh lemon, parsley and a hint of tarragon!

ingredients
1 tablespoon oil
1 onion, diced
2 carrots, diced
2 stalks celery, diced
2 cloves garlic, chopped
1 teaspoon thyme, chopped
4 cups chicken broth or chicken stock
2 cups cooked chicken, cut into small pieces
1 cup orzo (gluten free for gluten free)
salt and pepper to taste
1 lemon (zest and juice)
1 tablespoon tarragon, chopped (optional)
1 handful parsley, chopped

directions
1. Heat the oil in a large stock pot over medium-high heat, add the onions, carrot and celery and cook until tender, about 8-10 minutes.
2. Add the garlic and thyme and cook until fragrant, about a minute.
3. Add the broth, chicken and orzo, bring to a boil, reduce the heat and simmer until the orzo is just tender, about 5 minutes.
4. Season with salt and pepper to taste and mix in the, lemon juice, zest and parsley.

Note: I like to use the meat from the chicken that I used to make the chicken broth but you could use rotisserie chicken or leftover chicken from another dish. If you use raw chicken breasts, thighs, etc, cook them in the pot in some oil before step one.
Option: Mix in 1/4 cup finely grated parmigiano reggiano (parmesan) in at the last step.
Slow Cooker: Optionally implement step 1, place everything except the orzo, lemon, tarragon and parsley in the slow cooker and cook on low for 6-10 hours or high for 2-4 hours before adding the orzo, cooking on high until tender, about 10 minutes, and mixing in the lemon, tarragon and parsley. Another option is to use whole chicken breasts or thighs, placing them in the slow cooker with everything and pulling them out, shredding and returning to the soup when it is done cooking.

Nutrition Facts: Calories 172, Fat 3.2g (Saturated 0.5g, Trans 0), Cholesterol 27mg, Sodium 322mg, Carbs 20.5g (Fiber 2g, Sugars 3.2g), Protein 14.8g

Crispy Buttery Garlic Roasted Mushrooms

Prep Time: 5 minutes **Cook Time**: 20 minutes
Total Time: 25 minutes **Servings**: 4

Garlic and butter roasted mushrooms topped with crispy breadcrumbs!

ingredients
1 pound button mushrooms
1/4 cup butter, melted
2 cloves garlic, chopped
2 teaspoons thyme, chopped (optional)
salt and pepper to taste
1/2 cup panko breadcrumbs (or breadcrumbs;
    gluten-free for gluten-free)
1/4 cup parmigiano reggiano (parmesan), grated

directions
1. Place the mushrooms in a baking dish, spoon the mixture of the butter, garlic and thyme onto the mushrooms, season with salt and pepper.
2. Bake in a pre-heated 400F/200C oven for 10 minutes before sprinkling on the mixture of the breadcrumbs and parmesan and baking until lightly golden brown, about 8-10 minutes.

Option: Garnish with chopped parsley and hit the mushrooms up with a splash of lemon juice just before serving.

Nutrition Facts: Calories 182, Fat 13g (Saturated 8g, Trans 0.3g), Cholesterol 35mg, Sodium 115mg, Carbs 9g (Fiber 1g, Sugars 2g), Protein 6g

Mushroom and Peppercorn Crusted Steak in a Creamy Brie Mushroom Sauce

Prep Time: 10 minutes **Cook Time**: 20 minutes
Total Time: 30 minutes **Servings**: 4

Pan seared steak crusted in dried mushroom and fresh cracked peppercorns served topped with a velvety and creamy brie and mushroom sauce!

ingredients

FOR THE PEPPERCORN AND MUSHROOM CRUSTED STEAK:

1 tablespoon butter
1 tablespoon oil
1/4 ounce dried mushrooms, coarsely chopped in food processor
1 teaspoon fresh cracked peppercorns
salt to taste
1 pound ribeye steak (or tenderloin, or your favourite cut)

FOR THE CREAMY MUSHROOM SAUCE:

2 tablespoons butter
1 small onion, diced
8 ounces various mushrooms, sliced
2 cloves garlic, chopped
1 teaspoon thyme, chopped
1/4 cup dry white wine (or beef broth)
1/4 cup beef broth
1/4 cup heavy/whipping cream
4 ounces brie (optionally with the rind removed)
1/2 cup parmigiano reggiano (parmesan), grated
1 tablespoon white miso paste (optional, gluten-free for gluten-free)
salt and pepper to taste

directions

FOR THE PEPPERCORN AND MUSHROOM CRUSTED STEAK:

1. Melt the butter and heat the oil in a pan over medium-high heat, press the mixture of the dried mushrooms, peppercorns and salt into the steaks and cook in the pan to the desired level of doneness, about 2-4 minutes per side, before letting sit for 5 minutes before optionally slicing and serve topped with the mushroom sauce!

FOR THE CREAMY MUSHROOM SAUCE:

2. Add the onions and mushrooms to the pan and cook until the mushrooms release their liquids and it's absorbed, about 10-15 minutes.
3. Add the garlic and thyme and cook until fragrant, about a minute.
4. Add the wine and deglaze the pan.
5. Add the broth and cream, bring to a boil and simmer to thicken, about 2-4 minutes, before mixing in the cheeses and miso and removing from the heat.

6. Season with salt and pepper to taste.

Nutrition Facts: Calories 582, Fat 46g (Saturated 22g, Trans 1g), Cholesterol 140mg, Sodium 467mg, Carbs 6g (Fiber 1g, Sugars 2g), Protein 34g

About Nutrition Facts

The nutritional facts were calculated using automated tools and they should be considered to be estimates. If you have any dietary requirements based on the nutrition facts you should calculate them yourself using a trusted source, using the nutrition facts of the ingredients and brands of products that you use in the recipes.

Other Cookbooks by Closet Cooking

Summer Salads

Tasty Soups

Melty Grilled Cheese

Game Day Party Food

The Best of Closet Cooking 2012

The Best of Closet Cooking 2013

The Best of Closet Cooking 2014

The Best of Closet Cooking 2015

The Best of Closet Cooking 2016

More Recipes

If you liked these recipes, you can find more on ClosetCooking.com

The Best of Closet Cooking 2017

Made in the USA
Columbia, SC
26 December 2023

29442915R00024